Editors Lesley Firth
       Dale Gunthorp
Design Patrick Frean
Picture Research Mary Walsh
Production Rosemary Bishop
       Vivienne Driscoll
Illustrations Hayward Associates
       Patrick Frean
       Tony Payne
       John Shackell
Maps Matthews and Taylor Associates
Consultant Frank E. Huggett

First published 1976
Macdonald Educational Ltd.
Holywell House, Worship Street,
London E.C.2.

© Macdonald Educational Ltd. 1976

ISBN 0 356 05273 7

Made and printed by
Waterlow (Dunstable) Limited

Colour reproduction by
Fotomecanica Iberico, Madrid

The cover shows the flower market in the Grand' Place, Brussels.

The endpaper shows Viandey Castle in Luxembourg.

Page 6 shows a street scene in Bruges, Belgium.

Belgium and Luxembourg

the lands and their people

Joan and George Morey

Macdonald Educational

Contents

Belgium's golden age

A divided nation

The kingdom of Belgium came into being in 1831, but the region that we now know as Belgium has a long, interesting history going back to Roman times.

Belgium is a country with no natural frontiers, apart from a short coastline. It has three official languages: French, Dutch and German. Its biggest problem is that the country is divided between the Flemings, who speak Dutch, and the Walloons, who speak French.

In recent years the differences between these two groups have developed into public quarrels. Despite their differences, the Belgians have a sense of national unity. For example, the Flemings and Walloons will join together to support the Belgian football team in international matches, and everyone was delighted when the Belgian cyclist Eddy Merckx won the Tour de France!

◄ Charlemagne (742-814 A.D.), first Holy Roman Emperor. He was one of the founders of Western civilization after the fall of Rome. Belgium was part of his empire, which covered a large area of Europe.

▼ The Cloth Hall, Ypres. The original building was built in the Middle Ages when Ypres was important for the trade in woollen cloth. The Cloth Hall was destroyed in World War I. It has been rebuilt to look like the original building.

The Middle Ages

In the past, Belgium has often been fought over and divided by foreign armies. The Belgians were sometimes able to turn this position to their advantage. In the Middle Ages, towns such as Ypres, Ghent and Bruges won wealth and fame as centres of trade and industry although Belgium was ruled by foreign overlords.

Belgium's great days lasted only from the twelfth until the early fifteenth century. During that time, many fine buildings were erected and the Flemish school of painting flourished.

Decline began as rival nations rose to power. The decline became rapid when the Dutch rebelled against the Spaniards, who then ruled the Low Countries. The Belgians joined in revolt against the Spaniards, but were defeated and severely punished. It was not until the nineteenth century that Belgium began to thrive again.

▲ *Peasants Dancing* by Pieter Brueghel the Elder (c. 1525-69). Many of his paintings have survived, and give a brilliant idea of how ordinary Flemish people lived in the 16th century. The picture shows peasants enjoying one of the many religious holidays

▲ The Grote Markt at Bruges, with its famous belfry. Bruges was an important trading centre in the Middle Ages.

◄ Philip the Good, Duke of Burgundy (1419-67) hearing Mass. He did much to encourage the arts in the Low Countries.

Giovanni Arnolfini and his wife by Jan van [Eyck] (c. 1390-41). This gives a good idea of the interior of a rich Flemish house [and the way people dress]ed. The Belgian cities were so important at [that] time that many Italian merchants lived [there].

The land
of Belgium

Varied scenery

Belgium is a small country. It is not much bigger than Wales or Maryland. The boundaries are never further than 322 km. (200 miles) apart. Belgium is also one of the most thickly populated countries in Europe, so that in many parts of the country one is never very far from a house. The motorist, who dashes across Belgium on his way elsewhere, sees the least interesting part of the country and misses a great deal.

For so small a country, the scenery is very varied. In the north-west, the dykes and polders which protect the land from the sea, and the canals and watercourses which drain the low-lying fields, recall the landscape of the Netherlands. The highest ground, and the most thickly wooded areas, are to be found in the Ardennes, which include much of southern Belgium.

Belgium is not naturally a rich and fertile land. Its climate is colder and damper than that of the British Isles. It is said to rain on more than 200 days a year. The hard work of generations of peasants has made the land productive.

North of the French border, the distr around Mons and Charleroi serves as reminder that Belgium is a highly ind trialised country. This is only one of number of industrial centres. The surrour ings are scarcely different from what is be seen in northern France.

Flanders

The scenery quickly changes as one mo into Flanders. The Flemish houses are of built of red brick and have high-pitch roofs. They have iron roller-shutters at windows which, when lowered, often g the odd impression that the village deserted!

A curious thing is that the houses, of designed to stand in terraced rows alon street, are instead built in ones and tw This gives the owners more privacy, bu adds greatly to the cost of the house. It is necessary to go far in Flanders before see some of the new factories, many forei owned, which are bringing prosperity.

A country of contrasts

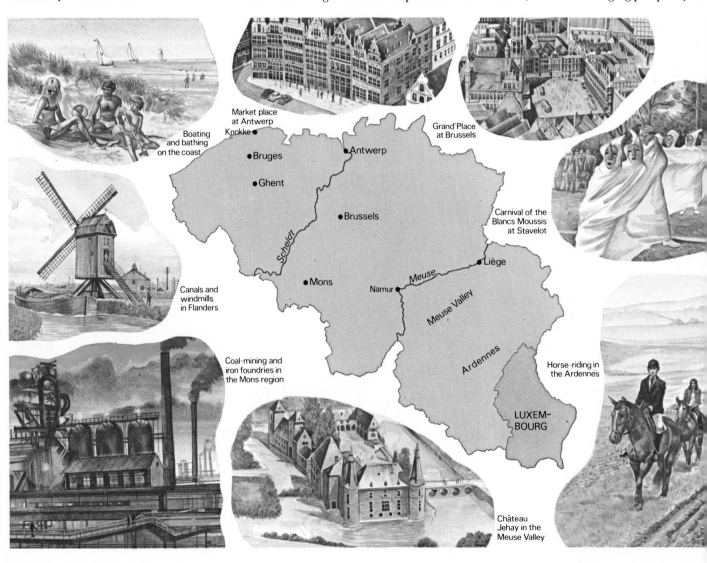

Boating and bathing on the coast

Market place at Antwerp

Grand'Place at Brussels

Canals and windmills in Flanders

Carnival of the Blancs Moussis at Stavelot

Coal-mining and iron foundries in the Mons region

Horse-riding in the Ardennes

Château Jehay in the Meuse Valley

Knokke • Bruges • Ghent • Antwerp • Brussels • Mons Namur • Liège

Scheldt

Meuse

Meuse Valley

Ardennes

LUXEM-BOURG

One of the many beautiful canals in
[Brid]ges. A trip by motor boat offers an
[exce]llent way of seeing the fine old houses.
[Brid]ges gets its name from the many bridges
[whi]ch cross the canals.

▲ Farmland in the Ardennes. Some of the
best cattle-raising country is found where
forest land has been cleared. Belgium's
white-blue and red-white cattle deserve to
be better known abroad.

▼ Brussels by night. The Grand' Place, at the
centre of the oldest part of Brussels, is floodlit
at night. The 17th century houses around the
square are dominated by the belfry of the
Town Hall.

▲ The Freyr Rocks, near Dinant. The valley of
the Meuse south of Dinant has some of the
most attractive scenery in Belgium. The
limestone hills on its right bank dominate a
gently flowing river which attracts many
visitors during the summer.

Luxembourg and its people

An important place in history

The Grand Duchy of Luxembourg is smaller than Cornwall or Rhode Island. With such powerful neighbours as France, Germany and Belgium, it is surprising that Luxembourg survived in times past, but it has an independent ruler, and the people speak a dialect of their own.

Luxembourg has had an important place in history. Four of its rulers became emperors of the Holy Roman Empire. The end of Luxembourg seemed to be near in the last century. In 1815, it was given to the Dutch King. Then, in 1831, after Belgium had revolted against the Dutch, the Belgians acquired a large part of Luxembourg, which they have kept as the county of Luxembourg. The Germans and French, too, were always anxious to acquire the land.

Wine and steel

Luxembourg is a beautiful country. The northern half is wooded and hilly; the southern is fine agricultural land and produces wine. On the extreme southern edge is a small, but very important industrial area, producing a great deal of steel. Luxembourg industry is important today because of the work of a Briton, Sidney Gilchrist Thomas. Luxembourg has a lot of iron ore, but it was useless for steelmaking because it contained phosphorous. Gilchrist Thomas found a way to remove the impurities, and a great industry was born, which ensures the Luxembourgers a very high standard of living.

European unity

Luxembourg is very proud to have shown Europe the way to unity. In 1921, it entered into a customs union with Belgium. After World War II the Netherlands was included, to form Benelux. Luxembourg was one of the founder members of the Common Market. The European Court meets in Luxembourg, and some of the departments of the Common Market have their offices there.

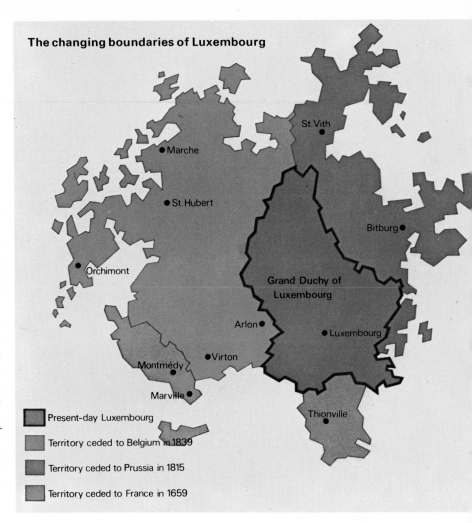

The changing boundaries of Luxembourg

Present-day Luxembourg

Territory ceded to Belgium in 1839

Territory ceded to Prussia in 1815

Territory ceded to France in 1659

▲ Luxembourg's changing boundaries. Her lands have often been sought by neighbours. The biggest change occurred after 1831, when a large area was given to Belgium.

▼ H.R.H. the Grand Duke Jean of Luxembourg with his family. The Grand D succeeded in 1964, when his mother abdicated after reigning for 45 years.

uxembourg City. Part of the city has been
around steep river gorges. The city has
idges, the biggest being the Grand
hess Charlotte Bridge.

cafe scene in Luxembourg City. The city
ys a warmer and drier climate than much
ighbouring Belgium. It is often possible
mmer to spend an hour with friends in an
air cafe.

ervaux Castle. The old turreted castle
uilt in the 16th century by the powerful
ts of Lannoi. It was severely damaged in
, but has been restored.

iron foundry in southern Luxembourg.
mbourg owes much of its prosperity to
In 1973, it produced nearly 6 million
of crude steel.

Family life

Belgian families and the law

Many Belgians, like the French, keep their home life private. You would probably have to know a Belgian family for a long time before being invited to spend an evening in their home. Even close friends often prefer to entertain one another in a restaurant. Attitudes are changing, but old ideas still persist.

Within the home, family ties are strong, and the law makes them stronger still. It is not unusual to find the old grandmother occupying part of a house, while her son and his family occupy the rest. This is not entirely a matter of kindness. The law gives her the right to a share of the old home.

Many of the older terraced Belgian houses are surprisingly narrow, and this often means that a house is three rooms deep. The owners get over the problem of lighting the room in the middle, without windows, by a skilful use of mirrors. The reason for this narrowness is that the householder is responsible for the pavement outside the house. If a passerby injures himself because the pavement is not properly kept, the householder is held responsible, and so he keeps his frontage as narrow as possible.

Now that so many foreigners live in Belgium, foreign ideas of house building are becoming better known. It is incr ingly common in the more expen suburbs to find bungalow-type houses flat roofs, and fine front gardens.

Inside the home

For many people, the Belgian living r in winter would be much too hot, for big radiators would be fully on. Belgians have a morbid fear of "a cur of air" and even in summer windows likely to be closed, and the curtains dra

Everyone is impressed by the numbe houseplants to be found even in the poo houses, and also by the cleanliness good order. The tiled floors of the o houses make it easy to take a bucket mop and wash the rooms right through.

The journey homewards from begins about 4.30 p.m. This leaves a evening, which the family often sp together.

▼ A Luxembourg farming family eats lunch in the fields. When the weather is fine, the farmer spends every possible moment working. When they are on holiday from school the children lend a hand.

A working class family budget

Food consume at home

Tobacco and drin consumed at home

Shoes and clothi

Rent, rates, electri gas and other fue

Household dur articles

Private cars a public transp

Entertainment restaurants, ca

Other expense

Bulletin de statistique, Brussels

▲ Manual workers in Belgium spend proportionately much more than office workers and managers on food and drink less on rent and entertainment. Food and take nearly half a pensioner's income.

Belgian family at table in their Brussels
Many Belgian families have their main
at mid-day, if they are able to travel
e.

◄ The Brussels street in which the family
lives. Many Belgians prefer houses to flats. It
is easier to find a home to live in than in most
other countries.

▼ The family relaxes together in the evening.
This family is wealthier than many Belgian
families, and is able to afford a very
comfortable home.

▲ The young son of the family doing his
homework. He is fortunate in having a place
of his own in which to work undisturbed.
Most parents are interested to see that
homework is well done.

Leisure and pleasure

Increased leisure time

The Belgians have a reputation for hard work, relieved only at intervals by bouts of noisy, exuberant fun. In fact, people in paid jobs have benefited by reduced hours, so that a forty-hour week is common for many workers.

There is nothing to prevent a person from taking a second job in his leisure time. However, for many workers, it means more time for their racing pigeons, rabbits and plants, or for a quiet drink and talk with their friends. The high cost of labour has also meant that the "do-it-yourself" movement has made big strides in Belgium.

Young Belgians often make use of their free time by riding around the countryside on their cycles, and going to the cinema, or on organised trips. Many take part in events arranged locally by young people.

Wealthier Belgians use their cars for trips into the countryside, or for visiting relations. They see their leisure time also as an opportunity to read or study, to talk to friends, as well as to watch television.

For many Belgians, Friday evening, out of season, is the signal to pack the car for a weekend at a hotel on the coast, where they will find sumptuous meals and have an opportunity to gamble at the local casino.

▼ Belgium, like many European countries, has a State lottery, with prizes every month. Many people find the hope of sudden riches hard to resist, especially as the draw approaches.

▲ A camp site on the River Sûre, Luxembourg. There are many similar sites in rural holiday areas. Campers often spend a great deal on their equipment, and insist that the camp is kept in very good order.

► Cafes on the Grand' Place, Brussels. These attract thousands of visitors, who enjoy the finest scene in old Brussels. During the week, the flower market in the square makes a colourful scene, and on Sundays there is a bird market. Belgians usually leave these cafes to the tourists.

...he casinos at some of the more famous ...day centres such as Spa, Ostend and ...kke, attract many visitors. In winter, ...e Belgians include a visit to the gaming ...s in a weekend's relaxation.

▲ A sailing lesson for young people in Ostend harbour. When the beginners know how to manage the sails, the boat is taken out into the sea. In calm weather this is an ideal place to learn.

▲ Hikers walking in the Ardennes. The region offers some of the finest walking country in Europe. The hills are not very high, but it is possible to get wonderful views over the surrounding countryside. At every holiday centre there is a fine choice of walks.

◄ The seashore at Blankenberge. Blankenberge has grown from a small fishing village into one of the most important seaside resorts in Belgium. Its special attraction is the long, sandy beach. At low tide, it is wide and safe for bathing.

A variety of sports

► Football is a very popular sport in Belgium, and there are hundreds of clubs. People watch the fortunes of foreign clubs closely, and if a Belgian club beats one of them the excitement is great.

Armchair sportsmen

Many Belgians are keenly interested sport, but most of them prefer to read ab it, or watch it, rather than take part th selves. A recent survey showed that, average, a Belgian spent only 6 minut day at sport. Since this figure inclu professionals and young men and won it means that many spent no time at a sport.

A good football match, or a local c race, will always draw a crowd of spectat since these are the favourite sports. But average Belgian, who is probably tire the end of the week, and not always when he will be free, often likes to take in sports which call for little organizatio

Belgium's many fine rivers provide ex lent sport and the best spots are often li with keen fishermen. The Belgians h borrowed the game of *petanche* from French. This game can be played in a q

▲ Emile Puttemans leading in the 5,000 metres event at the Munich Olympic Gam Although he was unplaced then, he set up world record of 13 min. 13 sec. for the sam distance during 1972.

◄ Eddy Merckx wins the final sprint in the Swiss professional championship. In his te years as a professional, he has won 385 victories, and won the Tour de France five times in six years.

...her such as the town square. It is a form
...owls, played with heavy metal balls,
...tly bigger than cricket balls. *Pelote*,
...which is a mixture of tennis and hand-
..., can be played in streets and squares.

...ling

...gium offers everything from tennis and
...e racing to sand yachting, but the sport
...ch excites every young Belgian is cycling.
...gians have recently done exceptionally
...l in international competitions, and
...ry boy dreams of winning the Tour de
...nce, and beating the best riders of
...nce, Italy and Spain.

...elgium has never tried to win inter-
...onal honours by spending great sums
...tate money in training athletes, as some
...ntries have done. Even its soccer players
...not full-timers. They have their own
...during the week, and are paid match-
...ey when they appear for their club.

...igeons being released from baskets at the
...t of a race. The pigeons are sent by rail to a
...ant starting place, the first one home
...g the winner. A good racing pigeon is
...th a lot of money.

...ackie Ickx, Belgium's most famous
...ng driver. He has distinguished himself in
...rts car and Formula 1 racing on many
...e world's circuits as a driver for Ferrari,
...ra and Brabham-Ford.

...race on the Francorchamps circuit.
...rcorchamps is Belgium's most important
...track. Like Le Mans, it makes use of
...lic main roads in places. It is 14 km.
...iles) in circuit.

Francorchamps racetrack

Quarry
La Source
Pits
Blanchimont
Eau Rouge
Cottage
Haut de la Cote
Stavelot
Masta
Burnenville
Malmédy

Tradition in education

Church and State schools

Many Belgian children start going to school at the age of two or three years, but they do not have formal lessons, and school is not compulsory until the age of six.

Parents can choose whether to send their children to a Church school or to a State school. The cost of maintaining both types of school is met by the State, and both are organized on similar lines. In most Catholic schools, boys and girls are taught separately. There are as yet few comprehensive schools.

The primary schools have a five-day week, with Wednesday afternoons free. The secondary schools may choose between a five-day week, or a six-day week with Wednesday and Saturday afternoons off. Teaching is carried out in the language of the district.

Discipline and formality

The educational system of Belgium is in the process of being reshaped. In the meantime, a foreign visitor may well feel that education is formal, and discipline strict. There is little place for sport. The best equipped school have gymnasiums, but one is unlikely to find Belgian schools surrounded with acres of playing fields. Many schools are old-fashioned by modern standards, and may, at best, have an asphalt playground. Very often, because space is hard to find, or perhaps because of the "population bulge", schools are tucked away in unlikely buildings.

The Belgian school system

Nursery schools — 3-6 year

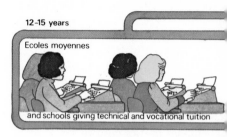

12-15 years

Ecoles moyennes

and schools giving technical and vocational tuition

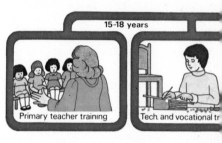

15-18 years

Primary teacher training — Tech. and vocational tr

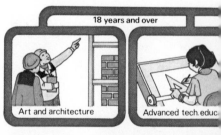

18 years and over

Art and architecture — Advanced tech. educ

▲ The beginning of another day at school. School buildings in Belgium often lack space for recreation. Frequent school trips to places of interest make up for lack of opportunity to play.

▶ A Belgian classroom. This is a school for girls only. Although big reforms in education are taking place, Belgian teaching methods are traditional, and discipline is strict.

imary schools   6-12 years

rammar schools   12-15 years

cée (girls) Athenée (boys)   General education

15-18 years

ducation   Grammar schools

18 years and over

r teacher training   University

▲ The gymnasium at the European School, Brussels. The school is intended for the children of Common Market officials, but others may join if places are available. Children are taught in their native language, plus one other E.E.C. language.

▼ Pupils in the science laboratory of a Belgian school. Generally, Belgian schools are less well equipped than they might be, because of the cost of satisfying differing requirements of Church and State schools, and Flemings and Walloons.

he University canteen at Louvain-le-ve. After the language riots in the 1960s, French faculties of Louvain University ed out to a new site at Ottignies.

Customs and carnivals

Keeping ancient customs alive

The Belgians love carnivals and processions, and enter into the spirit of the occasion with great enthusiasm. These festivities make a welcome break from hard work, and are occasions for family reunions.

The simplest processions, with flower-decorated cars and floats, interspersed with bands and parades of boys and girls in uniform, cost a great deal of money. Many of the events are far more elaborate. Although Belgium only became a kingdom in 1831, it has a long history and many events celebrate some important occasion in a town's history, or serve as a reminder of an ancient custom.

Some customs are so old that their origins are forgotten, and these must go back to pagan times. There are many tree legends. The Cracknel Festival at Geraardsbergen ends at nightfall with the ceremonial burning of a tree—a signal for the lighting of bonfires in the countryside around. However, it is hard to find a reason why, earlier in the day, the burgomaster and aldermen climb a little hill outside the town to drink a toast from a goblet of wine in which tiny fish are swimming around!

Religious origins

Some of the most important celebrations are religious in origin. One of the most important is the Procession of the Holy Blood at Bruges, when a crystal phial, said to contains drops of Christ's blood, is taken in procession.

A strange, but moving, spectacle is the Procession of the Penitents in the little town of Veurne, where people carry heavy crosses through the streets. The monks' robes which they wear, and the cowls over their heads, are very Spanish in character, and are a reminder that the Spaniards ruled Flanders for a long time.

Some people say that the carnivals are not what they were: that the motorcar has made it possible for people to meet together often and that people are becoming too sophisticated. But the carnivals continue to attract thousands.

▲ A guild festival in the Campine. The leaders wear the insignia of their office. S festivals make a pleasant break from routi in remote country districts.

◀ The Shrove Tuesday Festival of the Gil at Binche. During the procession, the Gill in their magnificent costumes, throw orar to the crowd.

▼ Veurne: the Procession of the Penitent This is held on the last Sunday in July. It i reminder of the Spanish occupation, whe Veurne was an important town.

Some famous Belgian festivals

▲ Fosse-la-Ville: In the mid-Lent carnival, the Chinels, whose costume reminds one of Mr. Punch's, dance through the street.

▲ Bruges: Procession of the Holy Blood. On Ascension Day, the return of the Crusaders with their Holy Relic is re-enacted.

▲ Ostend: Blessing of the Sea. All the ships are beflagged, and sound their sirens in response to the Blessing.

▲ Geraardsbergen: the Cracknel Festival is held on the last Sunday in February, on a small hill outside the town.

Ath: Procession of the Giants. The dding of the giant, Goliath, takes place on last Saturday in August. This is followed t day by a procession when the wicker-rk giants "dance" through the streets.

▲ St. Severin-en-Condroz: Christmas Nativity Play. The play takes place in the village church, and village children take part.

▲ Mons: Battle of the Lumeçon. At the end of the procession, St. George takes up the fight with the dragon, the Lumecon.

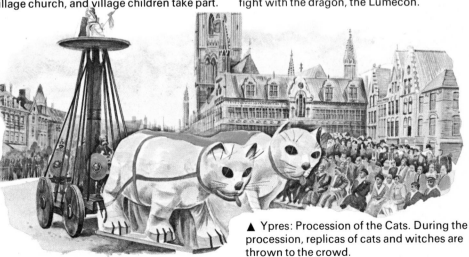

▲ Ypres: Procession of the Cats. During the procession, replicas of cats and witches are thrown to the crowd.

Patronage in the arts

Flemish art

Between the time of Jan van Eyck and Paul Rubens, the Flemish School produced some of the world's greatest art. At the same time Flemish architects were designing buildings of lasting beauty. The Low Countries were fortunate in producing artists of genius at a time when there were rich citizens who could support them with commissions.

The arts today

In modern Belgium, the place of the rich merchant has been taken over by business firms and the State. The Banque Lambert has one of the best collections of modern art in Belgium. The State, for example, by subsidizing Jeunesse Musicale and the Queen Elizabeth International Musical Contest, has done much to promote musical studies.

In music and the theatre, finances are more difficult. The opportunity to earn bigger fees in Paris and Amsterdam has attracted the best Belgian talent.

People who would like to do something for the theatre have been faced with three problems: general indifference on the part of the public, the language problem, and the readiness of Belgians to take, at second-hand, what has been produced abroad.

In these circumstances, the work at the Opéra de la Monnaie in Brussels, of Maurice Béjart and his ballet company, and of young groups like Internationale Nieuwe Scene, is a great achievement.

▲ *Christ, St. John, an angel and a little gir* by Paul Rubens (1577-1640). Rubens wa greatly influenced by his years of study in Italy, and became one of the greatest pain of his age. His fine house in Antwerp beca a meeting place for many distinguished people. It is now a museum.

▲ *Self Portrait* by James Ensor (1860-1949). Ensor was an Englishman, who later became a naturalized Belgian. His paintings of grotesque masks and animated skeletons, and his other Expressionist works, had a great influence upon other Belgian artists.

▶ A scene from *The Ballad of the Big and Small Puppets* presented by the young Antwerp theatre company, Internationale Nieuwe Scene. Their lively presentations have won praise even from critics who do not always approve of the social message of their plays.

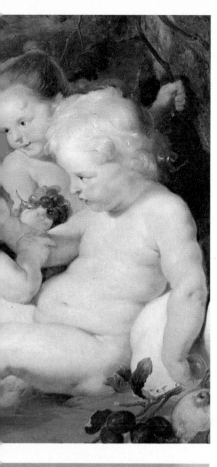

▲ A scene from Maurice Béjart's presentation of Stravinsky's *Firebird*. Although Béjart is a Frenchman, he works in Brussels, and has given his group an international reputation.

► César Franck (1822-90) was Belgium's greatest musician. His many works include Symphonic Variations for piano and orchestra. He worked mainly in Paris.

◄ Detail from *La Méditation* by René Magritte (1898-1967). Like many Belgian painters, Magritte was a surrealist.

▼ *The Conjurer* by Hieronymus Bosch (1480-1516). A group of peasants watches as a conjurer does the thimble trick. Much of Bosch's work is symbolic.

Shops and markets

Small shops

The small shopkeeper has an important place in Belgian life. Such businesses are often open for long hours, and sell things which nobody else would bother to stock.

Such shopkeepers have not had an easy time. In 1975, they called a one-day strike when the Government pegged prices. A few years ago they were ordered to close for at least one day each week, and for two weeks in the summer. At the same time, the law restricting the growth of big multiple shops was repealed.

Some of the small grocers have been able to help themselves by introducing self-service, and by forming into groups, which can take advantage of bulk buying. The small delicatessens continue to flourish. It makes one hungry to look at the prepared food in the windows!

One type of shop which seems to h escaped the move to modernization is chemist's. Some shops, even in the ce of Brussels, do not seem to have change a hundred years. One half expects chemist to grind up some powders and m some pills on the spot instead of produ modern manufactured medicines.

Markets and supermarkets

The many open air markets, to be foun streets and squares of many towns, a feature of Belgian life. Some of the best freshest fruit and vegetables can be bou there. However, the big stores and su markets continue to grow. Often there giant store on the edge of town, with r for many cars. The shopping centre Woluwe even has a church among facilities.

▼ A shop selling prepared game birds. Such shops are also likely to sell the delightful meat patés, of which there are several varieties. Belgian food shops maintain very high standards.

▲ A lace shop in Bruges. In summer, ma old ladies sit at their doors enjoying the s as they make their lace. It is fascinating to watch as they move the bobbins about to produce the patterns.

◀ A Brussels "flea market". The most far of these is in the Place du Jeu de Balle, in Les Marolles quarter, and is open every morning. Here one is likely to find anythi clothes, ornaments, books, antiques, and sometimes a bargain. Whether one buys not, the flea market is always interesting.

▲ One of the many fine vegetable markets in Brussels. Housewives find the journey worthwhile because the produce is usually fresh and fairly cheap.

◄ Some Belgian currency. This money can be used in Belgium and Luxembourg, although Luxembourg money is not readily accepted in Belgium. Coins are issued for values of 10 francs down to $\frac{1}{4}$ franc.

▲ A check-out point in a Belgian supermarket. Supermarkets are to be found in all the larger towns. The notice in Flemish (above) asks customers to help the cashier by having their money ready.

◄ The Galeries St. Hubert in Brussels. This is the most beautiful of all the Brussels arcades, and the oldest in Europe. It is lined by fine shops. Since the weather in Brussels often discourages window-shopping, many of the new buildings have shopping arcades.

Eating the Belgian way

Belgian restaurants

Most Belgians delight in good food. They are prepared to spend a lot of money on a good meal, and in return expect generous helpings. Brussels has many restaurants. In some of the old streets, such as the Rue des Bouchers, the restaurants often stand side by side on both sides of the street.

Although rising costs limit the opportunities for eating out, the best restaurants continue to flourish. They are seldom very big, and in summer chairs and tables are sometimes set out in the middle of the street for late-comers. Away from the centre of Brussels, some good restaurants are in private houses, where the family has given over its best rooms as a restaurant.

Belgian cooking

Belgian cooking relies heavily upon dishes which the French have made famous. Occasionally, famous French chefs are invited by Belgian hotels to arrange a *weekend gastronomique*, but generally one would have to travel a long way to find Belgian restaurants which equal the best of the French. Belgians who can afford the cost take weekend trips to eat in Paris restaurants.

Belgium has fine dishes of its own. Its seafood is outstanding. Mussels are eate[n] huge quantities. They are often served in a savoury broth, and eaten with must[ard]. The waiter will pretend to be disappoi[nted] if you do not finish two big plate[s]. Another famous dish is *waterzooi*, made variety of fish served in a broth. Chic[ken] is often used instead.

Nearly every region has its speciali[ty] such as *porc à la St. Hubert* from the Arden[nes] which is especially good if wild boar [meat] is used, and *anguilles à la vert*—"green e[els]" a speciality of Antwerp.

Belgians drink a lot of beer. Much is of a lager type and is imported. [One] traditional Belgian beer is called *gu[euze]*. Another interesting beer is *kriek*, whi[ch is] flavoured with cherries.

Belgian seafood

▲ Oysters are a favourite dish, but they are rather expensive. Many are reared in the quiet backwaters of Zeeland.

▲ The Belgians have created many delicious fish soups. *Waterzooi* includes both fresh and salt water fish.

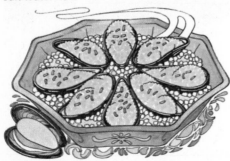

▲ Mussels are popular. One way of serving them is to grill them with breadcrumbs and grated cheese.

▲ A seafood stall. There are many such stalls in market places. This stall sells various kinds of shell fish, such as crabs, winkles and whelks. These can be eaten on the spot or taken home.

Make yourself a Belgian meal

ENDIVE WITH HAM

2 lb endive (chicory) heads
8 slices boiled ham
juice of 1 lemon
4 oz Gruyère cheese, grated
pinch of salt
water
white sauce

Wash and trim the endive heads. Put the[m] into a saucepan with the lemon juice, sal[t and] water. Boil for 15 minutes. In the meanti[me] make a white sauce as follows. Melt a kn[ob] of butter in a heavy pan and add enough plain flour to make a stiff paste. Graduall[y add] milk to the paste, stirring constantly so th[at it] thickens into a smooth white sauce. Sea[son] the sauce with salt and pepper. When the endive is cooked, drain it and press out excess water. Roll each endive head in a [slice] of ham and place it in a shallow oven-pr[oof] dish. Cover the endive and ham with the white sauce and sprinkle with grated che[ese]. Bake it in a moderate oven (Gas 4, Electricity 350°F) for 10 minutes.

◀ Fishing for shrimps on the Belgian coast. Fishermen ride horses, dragging the heavy nets, through the shallow waters.

▼ An evening meal in a popular Brussels restaurant. Nearly everyone has ordered mussels. Prices are high, but the best restaurants are very busy.

BONNADE OF BEEF

s stewing or braising steak
nions, chopped
nd pepper
utter or lard
t beef stock
t beer
lain flour
lespoon brown sugar

 any fat off the meat and cut it into
ks. Season with salt and pepper. Melt
utter or lard in a frying pan and brown
eat in it quickly. Remove the meat from
an. Add the chopped onions to the
pan and cook until soft. Place the
and onions in layers in a heavy stew-
Add the beer and some of the beef stock.
e flour into the fat remaining in the
pan and add the rest of the beef stock
y so that it thickens. Add the thickened
to the meat and onions in the stew-pan
eason with the sugar. Cover the pan and
gently for two hours. Serve with boiled
es and vegetables.

WHITE CHEESECAKE

6 oz flaky pastry
1 lb unsalted curd cheese
2 oz castor sugar
pinch of salt
1 oz flour
2 egg yolks
2 tablespoons softened butter
2 egg whites
sugar for glazing

Line a shallow eight-inch flan ring or pie dish with the pastry. Crumble the cheese into a large bowl and add the castor sugar, salt, flour, egg yolks and butter. Mix these together thoroughly. Whip the egg whites and gently fold them into the mixture. Fill the pastry case with the mixture. Bake in a hot oven (Gas 7, Electricity 425°F) for about 25 minutes, until the cheesecake is firm. Sprinkle the top of the cheesecake with sugar and raise the temperature of the oven (Gas 8, Electricity 450°F) for a few minutes to glaze the top.

▲ Gathering endives. Endives are exported all over Europe, where they are used in salads. Belgians originally grew chicory (endives) to mix the roots with coffee, and then found that the shoots were nice to eat.

29

Creating a kingdom

Belgian independence

After Napoleon had been defeated at Waterloo in 1815, it was felt that France should be prevented from threatening Europe again. Britain wished to prevent France from ever again winning control of Antwerp and the River Scheldt.

A Kingdom of the Netherlands which included Belgium was therefore created, with a Dutchman, Prince William, as King. The arrangement did not please the Belgians, who began to complain that they were being exploited. In 1830, they rebelled, and declared themselves independent. They were supported by Britain, and in 1831, Leopold of Saxe-Coburg was invited to become the first King of the Belgians.

The Dutch, at first, refused to recognise the new State, and nobody thought that it could last long. It seemed impossible to make a nation of two groups as different as the Walloons and the Flemings. The new country had only one natural frontier, and her neighbours seemed to be waiting for a chance to swallow her.

Belgium survived largely because of Leopold's diplomatic skill and the support which Britain gave. He began, in 1831, by persuading the Belgians to accept a very harsh treaty, when nothing better could be had. He understood that Belgium needed to become stable and economically strong. He was even ready to defy the British, at the time of the Crimean War, to maintain the principle that Belgium must remain neutral at all times. When Leopold died in 1865 the survival of Belgium was assured.

Leopold II

His successor, Leopold II (1865–1909) was welcomed to the throne as the first truly Belgian king. The nation at that time was involved in a great industrial and agricultural revolution. Leopold's ambition was to have a share in the development of Africa. In spite of opposition, he proceeded to acquire the Congo. Judged by the standards of the time, it was a brilliant stroke of business and diplomacy. It helped to make Belgium a rich and important nation.

▲ Waterloo, the Battle of Mont St. Jean, June 1815. The battle resulted in the final defeat of Napoleon. Until the last hour it was not certain that the British and their allies would be victorious.

▶ A statue of William II, King of the Netherlands (1840-49) in Luxembourg. Luxembourg remained the private possession of the Dutch Crown until 1890, when the present ruling family succeeded.

▼ Belgian insurgents attack Dutch troops in the Royal Park, Brussels, September 1830. This brought an end to the revolution, and the Dutch troops withdrew from the capital.

opold I taking the oath as King of the
ans in July 1831. Leopold, who had
a German prince before accepting the
e, was uncle of the future Queen
ria of Britain.

rike Evening, a painting by Eugene
nans. Belgian workers suffered great
ships during the industrial revolution of
9th century, and this led to many strikes
ock-outs.

▼ Leopold II (1865-1909). In his reign,
Belgium became a rich and important
country, largely by developing the resources
of the Congo. In spite of the ambitions of the
other great Powers, he was able to ensure
that Belgium enjoyed a long period of peace.

Belgium as a battleground

The First World War

The neutrality of Belgium had been guaranteed. However, it was well-known that Germany was considering the possibility of bypassing the French defences, in the event of war, by invading Belgium. On August 4th, 1914, German troops crossed into Belgium, and the world watched aghast as the new German guns crushed the Belgian defences.

Nearly all of Belgium was quickly overrun. The Belgians flooded the Germans out of trenches near the River Yser, and thus prevented them from capturing the last corner of Belgium. King Albert (1909–34) and his army remained to fight the Germans until the end of the war. Belgium suffered severely before the Germans were defeated in 1918.

The Second World War

War threatened again in 1939. In Belgium, disagreements prevented the planning of proper defences. When, therefore, Hitler invaded Belgium on May 10th, 1940, he found little to halt his drive. On May 28th, King Leopold of the Belgians surrendered, and it was left to the Belgian government and a few brave people to escape and continue the struggle.

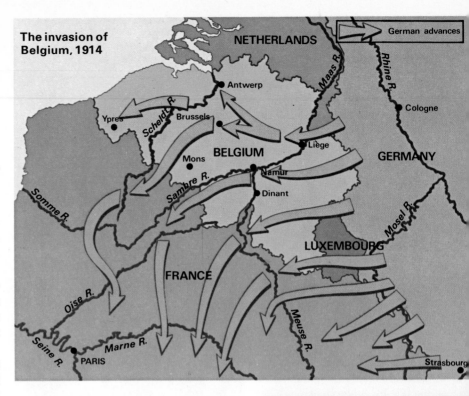

The invasion of Belgium, 1914

▲ The German advance through Belgium in World War I. Their intention to move quickly towards Paris was frustrated. Some of the heaviest battles were fought in Belgium.

▶ King Albert I (1909-34). By refusing to surrender, or to leave Belgium, Albert emerged as his country's hero.

▼ Belgian infantry moving up to the front during World War I. Although they could not hope to win, the Belgians managed to hold onto a small corner of their country.

▲ A war cemetery in Passchendaele. Around Ypres there are many cemeteries where soldiers of World War I are buried.

◄ British troops hauling a gun out of the mud in August 1917. Shell-fire destroyed the drainage system and made conditions terrible.

▼ German troops removing barricades after the surrender of Brussels, May 17th, 1940. The ease with which Belgium was conquered convinced the Germans that the war would be won quickly.

he magazine *Punch* published this ous cartoon in which the Kaiser taunts Albert with having lost everything. "But ny soul!" the King proudly replies.

Antwerp, a great port

The history of Antwerp

Although Antwerp lies 88 km. (55 miles) from the sea, on the banks of the River Scheldt, it is one of the greatest ports of Europe. In the Middle Ages, while Bruges flourished, Antwerp was no more than a river port. The storms which blocked up the entrance to Bruges, opened up the Scheldt to shipping.

This was very welcome to foreign merchants. They had always been more free to trade in Antwerp than they had been in Bruges. The time was also favourable. Neither France nor the Netherlands had the ports to handle the trade which was arriving from the Far East and the West Indies. By the beginning of the sixteenth century, Antwerp had a thousand foreign businesses dealing with Italy, Spain, and the rest of Europe. People could well say, "Antwerp owes the Scheldt to God, and everything else to the Scheldt".

This early prosperity did not last l[...] The Dutch rose in revolt against the Spa[...] overlords, and closed the Scheldt. W[...] the people of Antwerp tried to follow t[...] example, the revolt was severely crus[...] For many years after, the Dutch m[...] tained their stranglehold on Antwerp, [...] demanded heavy tolls from ships using [...] port.

Antwerp today

Since the Second World War, Antwerp [...] undergone great development. New [...] tories have sprung up, and the port [...] expanded across the river, and for m[...] miles downstream. The world's biggest l[...] at Zandvliet, enables big ships to enter. [...] need to link both river banks led to [...] building of the great Kennedy Tunne[...] great deal of the petroleum, upon wh[...] Belgian industry depends, is impo[...] through Antwerp.

◀ Antwerp is one of Belgium's greatest a[...] most interesting cities. The house of the painter, Rubens, and the workshop and house of the printer Christopher Plantin, a[...] particularly worth a visit.

▼ The Kennedy Road Tunnel. It links bot[...] banks of the Scheldt, which is here over $\frac{1}{4}$ mile wide. It was built, section by sectio[...] on dry land. The sections were then lowe[...] onto the bed of the river.

Places to visit in Antwerp

1 Rubens's House

2 Antwerp Cathedral

3 Brabo fountain in the Grote Markt

4 National Maritime Museum, Steen Castle

5 Zoological gardens

6 Sunday-morning bird market

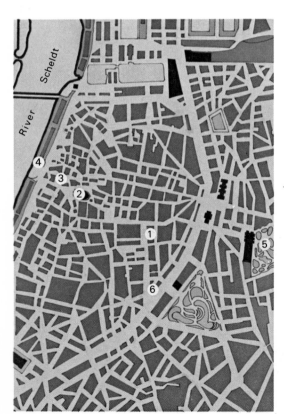

34

▲ Antwerp Cathedral. This is one of the biggest Gothic churches in the world. Although hemmed in by houses, the tall, delicate spire can be seen for miles.

◀ Antwerp Zoo lies just behind the Central Station. It contains one of the largest collections of rare animals and birds to be found in Europe.

▼ The port of Antwerp stretches for several miles along the river. The Scheldt is wide enough and deep enough to enable all but the biggest ships to reach it, and to make Antwerp one of the world's most important ports.

Language and media

The languages of Belgium

After the Romans withdrew in the century, the desolated lands in the nort Belgium were occupied by tribes of Ger origin, who spoke a different language f the Belgian tribes in the south.

Today there is still no single Bel language. In the north, the Flemings s various Dutch dialects, and Dutch is official language. In the south, the loons speak French.

The language frontier

There was a time when all official bus was done in French, and nobody gain senior job without a perfect knowledg French, even in the Dutch-speaking an The rights of the Dutch speakers have established only with difficulty. By fixi language frontier across the country 1962–3, the Government made it diff to arrive at any other solution. The e ence of two principal languages is an ex sive nuisance to a small country.

Belgium has a great many newspap of which the biggest are *Le Soir* and *Laatste Nieuws*. The Catholic newspa *La Libre Belgique*, circulates between two language groups. Belgium also has television services, one broadcasting Dutch and the other in French.

▲ Notices and advertisements are almost invariably in both languages. This is time wasting and expensive, and can be very confusing for foreigners.

▼ Language riots at Louvain in January 1968. The university was bilingual, but Flemish students protested about the privileged position of the Walloons.

▲ A Brussels news kiosk. In addition to a wide selection of papers in French and Du there are enough foreigners to make it worthwhile selling foreign publications.

language frontier was established in
...um in 1962-3. To the north, Dutch is
...fficial language. In the south it is
...ch. Brussels is bilingual. There are two
...an-speaking regions in the east.

Belgian cafe with the menu in both
...h and French.

The Belgian language frontier

- German speaking
- Bilingual (Dutch and French)
- French speaking
- Dutch speaking

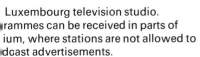

Luxembourg television studio.
...rammes can be received in parts of
...ium, where stations are not allowed to
...dcast advertisements.

A new role in Europe

The first steps to unity

Belgium emerged from the First World War more respected than ever before, and became one of the first signatories of the League of Nations. Belgium went on to point the way towards international cooperation by forming an economic union (B.L.E.U.) with Luxembourg.

The events of World War II encouraged thoughts of post-war cooperation, and in 1944 Benelux (an economic union of Belgium, the Netherlands and Luxembourg) was born. The early steps were not always easy because Belgian and Dutch interests were not always the same. But Benelux proved the value of cooperation, and in some respects progress was greater in Benelux than in later organizations.

The new Europe

The creation of a truly integrated Europe, which would include Britain, remained the cornerstone of Belgian policy. The steps towards it, such as defence agreements, the creation of the European Iron and Steel Community, and cooperation in the development of atomic energy, were welcomed. But these were all less important than the creation of the European Economic Community (the Common Market) by the Treaty of Rome in 1957. It was appropriate that the headquarters of the E.E.C. should be set up in Brussels.

Belgium took a further step towards becoming the centre of European decision-making in 1967. General de Gaulle ordered the two defence bodies SHAPE (Supreme Headquarters Allied Personnel Europe) and NATO (North Atlantic Treaty Oranization) to leave France. They both moved to Belgium. In the following year, the headquarters of the Iron and Steel Community, and of Euratom, were moved to Brussels.

Luxembourg, too, has had a share in these developments. It shares with Strasbourg the role of being host to the European Parliament. It also houses some sections of the E.E.C.

▲ A meeting of the North Atlantic Treaty Organization. Belgium willingly gave the Organization a new home after General de Gaulle ordered NATO to leave France in the Sixties.

▼ The United Kingdom joins the Common Market. The Prime Minister, Mr Heath, signed the Treaty of Accession in Brussels on January 22nd, 1972. Ireland and Denmark became members at the same time.

The European Community

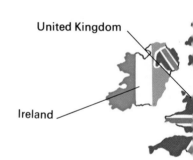

United Kingdom

Ireland

France

▶ The European Community was created by the six countries who signed the Treaty of Rome in March 1957. In 1972, the United Kingdom, Ireland and Denmark were also admitted. The Community aims at eventual union, and hopes to provide fair shares for all sections of society in the rising prosperity which co-operation would bring.

▼ The Berlaymont Building, Brussels. These offices house hundreds of officials drawn from all the nine member countries. Their job is to make proposals to the Council of Ministers, and to implement decisions.

▲ Judges in session at the European Court of Justice, Luxembourg. The Court is the supreme arbiter in deciding Community law.

▼ Signing the Treaty of Rome, March 25th, 1957. The treaty, signed by the leading ministers of "the Six"—Belgium, France, Germany, Luxembourg, Italy and the Netherlands—brought the Common Market into being.

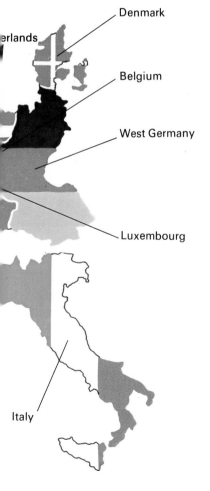

Denmark

Belgium

West Germany

Luxembourg

Italy

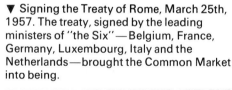

Old crafts and new skills

Steel, guns and glass

When World War II ended, the Belgians were quickly able to restore their industries, because their factories and transport system had suffered little damage. They found ready markets, and Belgium was very prosperous for several years.

However, new problems were arising. Belgium relied upon its old industries—especially coal and steel—and its old factories, while its neighbours were building new, efficient factories and new industries. In spite of this, Belgium remains a very important steel-making country. Two-thirds of its steel is sold abroad, and thousands of firms of all sizes are engaged in making everything from screwdrivers to locomotives.

One craft in which Belgium has established an international reputation is the manufacture of guns. The FN automatic rifle, developed in Belgium, has been adopted by several NATO countries.

Belgium has one of the biggest glass industries in the world. It developed because everything needed was at hand, including products from the important chemical industry. In some branches of glassmaking Belgium has led the world for many years.

Textiles and diamonds

Belgium's textile industry is concentrated mainly around Ghent and Verviers. Belgium's reputation for clothmaking goes back to the Middle Ages. In the manufacture of woollens, Belgium ranks second only to France among the European countries. She was also one of the first countries in the world to manufacture rayon, and now has an important synthetic trade.

The most interesting of Belgium's special trades is diamond cutting. This trade grew up in Antwerp, and the city has become the world centre for trade in cut diamonds. The less valuable diamonds are used by industry to make diamond-headed tools which are used on drills, for example, by the oil industry.

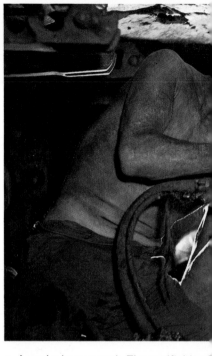

▲ A coal miner at work. The coalfields of Campine, north of Liège, contain 70% of Belgium's known reserves. Much of the electricity produced in Belgium comes fr[om] low-grade coal.

▼ A field of flax. Flax, from which the fin[e] Belgian linen is woven, is widely grown i[n] Flanders. It is the only natural textile whic[h] Belgium produces in quantities.

▲ A steel plant in Luxembourg. Luxembourg has rich supplies of iron ore. In Luxembourg and Belgium, steel making is the most important industry.

The Belgian crafts

Diamond cutting is centred in Antwerp. Antwerp is also the principal world centre for trade in cut diamonds.

▲ Lace making. Some of the lace sold in Belgium is manufactured at home, using old skills which have been handed down.

▼ Part of the oil terminal complex on the Scheldt at Antwerp. The port cannot handle the largest of the oil tankers now in service, but is ideally placed to process the crude oil used by industry.

Cutting patterns on crystal glass. Belgium makes high quality glass as well as flat glass. The craftsmen are very skilled.

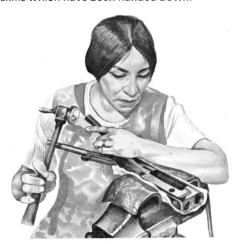

▲ Engraving a shotgun. The manufacture of guns is centred at Liège. Shotguns, used for sport, fetch a very high price.

From motorways to waterways

▼ In many Flemish towns it is often difficult to cross the road at rush hour because of the number of bicycles. Bicycles in Belgium have to be licensed.

Roads and ports

The giant lorries, rolling across Bel[gium] from all parts of Europe, the Middle [East] and beyond, make it clear that this i[s the] best route, and that Belgium is the c[ross] roads of Western Europe.

Antwerp, Zeebrugge, Ostend and G[hent] are four of Europe's most modern p[orts] handling many types of traffic. The m[otor] way, which crosses underneath the Sc[heldt] by the Kennedy tunnel, is part of the g[reat] system which will link northern Eu[rope] with the south.

Belgium's waterways and railway[s]

Belgium is fortunate in its rivers and ca[nals] which carry a great deal of traffic. For b[ulk] goods, which do not need to reach [their] destination quickly, the great river ba[rges] are ideal.

The Belgians have shown ingenuit[y in] solving difficult problems. On the Brus[sels-] Charleroi canal at Ronquières is the wo[rld's] only sloping lock. To overcome a [great] difference in waterlevel, ships are ca[rried]

▼ One of the most recent Belgian trains to be introduced. Its electrified main line service is very good. Its goods trains, which include several diesel locomotives, are very important to industry and trade.

▶ Barges on a Belgian river. In 1971, barges carried a record 95 million tons of freight. Belgium's river system is linked by canals which carry goods over a wide area of the Netherlands, Germany and France.

n one end of the lock to the other in two
e tanks of water which are hauled up
own the slope by powerful diesel engines.
elgium, which had the first railway on
European continent, now has one of the
sest railway networks in the world.

ving in Belgium

everywhere, Belgians buy cars because
like them, and they are useful, and they
demn everybody else's car for the
ance it causes! There was a time when
ians were considered the world's worst
ers, and the accident rate is still very
. But it is no longer possible to drive
out taking a test. It is a serious matter
e caught driving if drunk, and Belgium
ne of the first countries to make the
ring of seat belts compulsory.
he bicycle is still an important means of
ing about. Hundreds are to be seen
ed every day outside factories and at
way stations. Through the towns, and
g many roads, especially in Flanders,
cial paths have been laid for cyclists.

▲ A tram at one of Brussels' new
underground stations. The new Metro will
take several years to complete. In the meantime, trams run through the finished sections.
This saves much congestion on the roads.

▲ One of Belgium's motorways. The
motorway system, which has been built to
high standards, has made rapid progress in
the last decade. It is designed to form part of
the great European system.

▼ SABENA and LUXAIR are the national
air lines of Belgium and Luxembourg
respectively. SABENA is the bigger of the
two, and has some 70 overseas routes
serving 50 countries in four continents.
The size of Luxembourg airport puts
serious limitations on the size of aircraft
which LUXAIR can use.

Invention and discovery

Auguste and Jacques Piccard

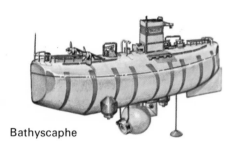

Bathyscaphe

▶ Professor Auguste Piccard (1884-1962) of Brussels University, was a pioneer explorer of the upper atmosphere and of the ocean depths. In 1931, he reached a height, by balloon, of 15,500 metres (50,853 ft.) and in the next year a record ocean depth. His son Jacques (1914--) reached a new record depth of 11 km. (7 miles) in the Pacific Ocean in 1960. To withstand the great pressures, he and his companion descended in a specially constructed bathyscaphe.

The development of industry

By the middle of the nineteenth cent Belgium had become an industrial nat and was taking an important part in development of new processes. Altho the names of some of the inventors are well-known, their work was important, sometimes led to the development of Belgian industries.

One such person was Ernest Solvay, developed a soda manufacturing proce 1863, which still bears his name. At a the same time, Daniel Dony, a L chemist, developed a new method separating zinc. Today, Belgium is am the world's leading exporters of non-fer metals. Better known is the work of L Baekeland, who invented bakelite, a f of moulded plastic.

Belgian researchers

In modern science, many researchers usually working in the same field. Zé Gramme (1826–1901), who built the industrial dynamo, was engaged in rese which made the name of the Gern Siemens, even more famous.

Etienne Lenoir, whose monument ca seen in Arlon, made important discov in the development of the petrol engine, another thirty years went by before Germans Daimler and Benz put the p engine into a motor car.

Mercator's projection

▲ Gerard Mercator, born in Rupelmonde in 1512, is famous as a mapmaker. Mercator's projection "flattened" the globe by making cuts from the Poles towards the Equator. Some countries look much too big, but the important parts of the world of his day were least distorted.

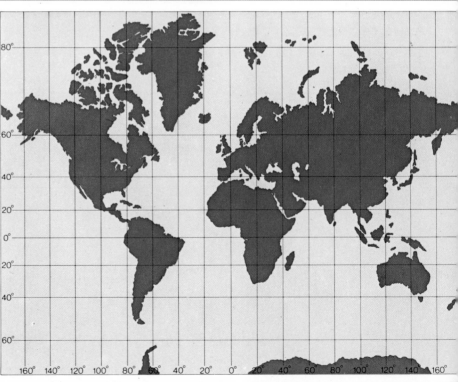

olphe Sax (1814-94), the inventor of
xophone, was born in Dinant. His
st saxophone was very different from
used by orchestras now, but the
ple was the same.

Vesalius

▼ Vesalius (Andreas van Wessels, 1514-64) turned the study of anatomy into a science. He rejected the notion that the ancient Greeks knew everything about the human body. His great work, *De Humani Corporis Fabrica,* was based on his own observations.

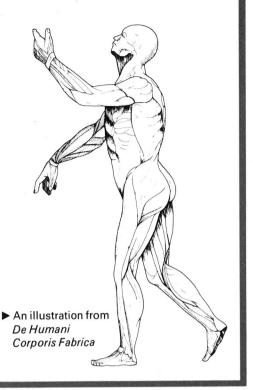

► An illustration from *De Humani Corporis Fabrica*

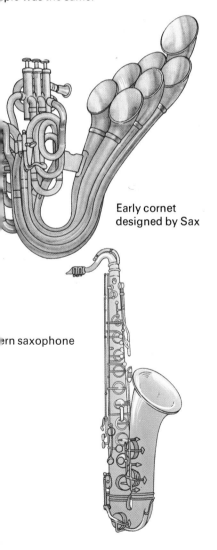

Early cornet designed by Sax

rn saxophone

Christopher Plantin

▼ The Plantin Museum, Antwerp. Christopher Plantin (c.1520-89) founded one of the greatest printing houses of his period. His masterpiece was a polyglot Bible. The modern typeface named after him (right) is based on one of his.

abcdefghijklmnop
qrstuvwxyz
ABCDEFGHIJKLMNO
PQRSTUVWXYZ
1234567890 .,;:?!-'&£

Heroes in fact and fiction

▼ The Toone Puppets. The puppet theatre is hidden away in a narrow alley in the oldest part of Brussels. The play, which is changed every month, is performed in a local dialect.

Early leaders

The Belgians have always had great ad[mira]tion for leaders who have roused the pe[ople] to defend themselves against the enem[y.] Tongeren, a fine statue of Ambiorix st[ands] in the main square. It was he who le[d the] tribes of the Belgae in revolt agains[t the] Romans.

Godfrey of Bouillon, whose castle [can] still be seen in the Ardennes, earned [fame] as a leader of the First Crusade. He [was] elected King of Jerusalem in 1099, [but] refused to wear a golden crown in a [city] where Christ wore a crown of thorns.

Heroes of the people

Although he was much less famous, m[ost] Belgians know about Everard t'Ser[claes] (1320–88). He was a deputy mayo[r of] Brussels, who was murdered while de[fending]

▲ Cardinal Mercier, Archbishop of Mali[nes] (1851-1925) took a leading part during the First World War in building Belgian morale to resist the enemy. The Germans did not dare to imprison him, as a leading churchman.

◄ Interior of the Erasmus House, Brusse[ls]. The great scholar paid frequent visits to Brussels, and from about 1525 stayed in [this] house, which belonged to his friend Can[on] Wichmann. The house is now a museum [of] Erasmus's life and works.

e city. During the Second World War,
German troops occupied Brussels,
le made a practice of visiting his
ument, and touched the brass figure as
rk of respect. Today, hundreds of
rs come to the site, and continue to
the figure for luck.
e First World War produced national
s. Adolphe Max, the Mayor of Brussels,
ly encouraged people to defy the
nans for a whole month before he was
ted and sent to prison. His place was
by Cardinal Mercier, Archbishop of
nes, who ordered the priests to read
letter calling upon people to support
King and ignore the enemy. He kept
German governor standing whenever
alled, and it was only in November
, when Germany had been defeated,
he offered the Governor a chair.

▲ Tintin and his dog. This famous cartoon
character was created by the Belgian artist,
Hergé. Since he first appeared, his adventures
have been followed in newspapers, books,
and on television by children everywhere.

► Georges Simenon, who was born in Liège,
wrote a series of detective novels featuring
the famous character Inspector Maigret.
Many of the novels have been dramatized.
On the right is a scene from a television
series in which the actor Rupert Davies
played the part of Inspector Maigret.

dolphe Max drinks a glass of beer with
Albert after the Germans had been
n out of Belgium. As deputy mayor of
els, he had been imprisoned in 1914
lling on the population to resist the
ans.

e monument to Everard t'Serclaes, near
er of the Grand' Place, Brussels, is
d by many people. The brass figure, and
ose of his dog, have become shiny
e people have touched them to bring
luck.

The Belgian character

A middle class society

There are very rich Belgians, and there are very poor ones, too. But Belgian society is above all middle class. There is a Minister for the Middle Classes in the Government.

As a nation, Belgians are very hard-working. They believe in giving, and getting, good value. They often seem to be interested only in material things. For many people everyday life may be dull, but when they get the opportunity to enjoy themselves, they enter into the spirit of it with great enthusiasm.

Conservatism and stability

According to the newspapers, Belgium appears to be beset with many problems and disputes, but it is really a very conservative country. New, small political parties attract attention from time to time, but it is really the three main parties who dominate the scene.

The great influence of the Catholic Church makes for stability. It affects people's ordinary lives, too. It is difficult

for a person, having chosen to belong [to a] party, to change his politics. Many [of the] things he does, such as the union he [belongs to,] and the club he belongs to, have their [links] with the Church and politics.

A nation of individualists

Most Belgians are individualists, prefe[rring] their own company and that of their [close] friends. This makes it difficult for forei[gners] to get to know Belgians socially. [This] attitude spills over into public life. S[ome] communities prefer to run their own af[fairs,] and most people are suspicious of autho[rity.] Life in Belgium, however, is changing [and] the attitudes of young people are often [very] different from those of their parents.

A contrast is often made betwee[n the] shorter, dark, volatile Walloon of the [south] and the taller, fair-haired, dour Flem[ing.] But this, in spite of their political differe[nces,] can be exaggerated. Intermarriage obs[cures] many differences. Above all, they are [Bel]gians, and when the honour and dign[ity of] their country is at stake, they react as o[ne.]

▼ To Belgians any current of air is a draught. In summer they would often prefer to swelter rather than open a window. Foreigners in Belgium look forward to the day when air conditioning is universal!

◄ Like the Germans, Belgians shake hands on every conceivable occasion. It would not be unusual for an office worker to shake hands all round with his colleagues in the room, and perhaps on some other occasion during the day as well.

▲ A Brussels flower market. The daily flower market in the Grand' Place is ope[n] from 9 a.m. to 4 p.m. With the gaily-colo[ured] umbrellas under which the traders sit, th[e] market makes a brilliant foreground to t[he] ancient buildings.

▲ A Sunday afternoon cycle race in a provincial town. Young men train hard for the honour of winning local races even when the prizes are small.

◀ The rush to get home. Belgians are not used to forming a queue, and tram entrances often get blocked. Oddly, people do not usually protest loudly when somebody cheats to get on.

▼ Good food matters a great deal to Belgians. During the low season, proprietors fill their hotels by arranging "gastronomic weekends". Celebrated chefs are invited to prepare special dishes. It costs much less to buy a bag of chipped potatoes or a waffle from a stall in the street.

The Belgian influence

The Flemish influence

Between about the thirteenth and sixteenth centuries, Flanders was the major centre of the artistic and commercial life of Western Europe.

The splendid cloth, which the Flemings wove from fine English wool, found buyers everywhere. Flemish towns grew to replace the great annual fairs, which had once met Europe's needs. The Flemish towns grew rich on two-way commerce, which reached to the most distant parts. Flemish seamen were feared, if not respected, over the whole of the North Sea.

The descendants of those who made money spent freely, and the wonderful architecture of the old towns and the art of the Flemish school are permanent heritages. In later years, when conditions in Flanders became difficult, many people from these parts carried their skills with them when seeking new homes in England and elsewhere.

In modern times, Belgium has played a part out of proportion to her size. Queen Victoria was particularly annoyed that the Belgians should have minds of their own. At one point, she wrote to the Belgian King, "I cannot at all see HOW you can *even* entertain the question, for, as I just said, the *basis* of the *existence* of Belgium is her neutrality".

The Congo

King Leopold II realized the importance and wealth of Africa at a time when European nations were content to establish trading posts. In 1885, with the advice of the explorer Stanley, Leopold established a vast colony in the Congo as his own private venture. The new colony was rich in rubber and ivory. In 1908, the Belgian government assumed responsibility for the Congo, following protests against the treatment of the native Congolese. The colony achieved independence in 1960.

It has been in Europe that her statesmen, such as Paul-Henri Spaak and Jean Rey, have helped Belgium to make her greatest contribution by promoting the unity of Western Europe.

▲ Assembling stained glass. Belgium has one of the biggest glass industries in the world. The industry includes the manufacture of blown-glass, crystal, and the design of stained glass.

▲ Jacques Feyder (1888-1948) the Belg film producer. In 1935, he produced the classic *Kermesse Heroïque*. As Belgium h no major film industry of its own, he worked in Paris.

▼ *Shepherds adoring the Lamb,* by Van Goes (c. 1445-82). His best work is in Florence. He would be better known as a Flemish painter if more of his paintings were in Belgium.

▲ Belgian merchants in the Middle Ages made the Low Countries among the richest areas in Europe. The fine woollen cloth they sold was prized everywhere.

◀ King Baudouin I and Queen Fabiola. Baudouin succeeded his father after the latter had been forced to abdicate. The Crown has since regained much of its respect.

▼ Patrice Lumumba and Joseph Kasavubu, respectively Prime Minister and Head of State of the Congo, following the granting of independence in 1960.

...aul-Henri Spaak (1899-1972), the first ...ident of the U.N. General Assembly. He ... twice Belgian Prime Minister, and six ...s Foreign Minister. He was an architect of ...pean integration.

Progress and prosperity

Non aux villes inhumaines!...

▶ One of many posters to be seen, urging Belgians to preserve and modernize old buildings instead of tearing them down to make room for tall office blocks.

▼ The Nuclear Energy Study Centre, at Mol, near Antwerp. It has three large reactors, and is designed to train specialists in nuclear research. It was founded in 1947 and employs some 1,200 staff.

The problems of prosperity

In Brussels great office blocks are b[...] built, and for a long time traffic has ha[...] cope with major roadworks in the [...] centre. These changes have done not[...] to make Brussels more beautiful, [...] essential changes have not always b[...] carefully planned. In many parts [...] Flanders, new factories with well-kn[...] foreign names are to be seen. This all po[...] to Belgium's growing prosperity, and t[...] new role in Europe.

Changes in Flanders

One big change has been more subtle. M[...] of the new industries have grown up in [...] Flemish area of the north, while the o[...] industries in the south have not shown [...] same progress. As their region has bec[...] richer and more important, the Fle[...] people have become more outspoken.

▲ Commuters arriving at the Central Rai[...] Station, Brussels, to begin another day's [...] work. Many people travel to the capital ea[...] day, attracted by the higher wages. The [...] development of Belgium's excellent railw[...] enables them to commute longer distance[...]

...he days when the Flemings were mainly
... labourers, and the French-speaking
...loons were better educated and able to
...mand the best jobs, have now gone.
... Flemings have won many important
...ts.

...v industries

...development of new industries has been
...d, and none has grown faster since the
... than the oil industry. Belgium's oil
...eries support an important petro-
...nical industry. Belgium has not been
... to move towards nuclear energy. Two
...e nuclear power stations are being
...loped at Doel and Tihange.

...elgium has always been a meeting place
...oreign people and foreign cultures. This
... today because of Belgium's growing
...ortance in international business and
...tics.

▲ An American-owned petroleum refinery
at Feluy, near Mons. This side of Belgian
industry has made very rapid progress since
the days when Belgium was merely a
distributor of imported gasoline.

▼ The Sidmar steelworks at Zelzate in East
Flanders. Scrap metal is being added to the
converter. Antwerp is conveniently near as a
source of iron ore and for the shipment of
finished products.

...Mealtime at a day nursery in Brussels.
...ny children up to the age of three can be
... at a day nursery if the mother goes out to
...k or is ill. Belgium has established a fine
...rd in providing such schools as part of
...ocial services.

Reference
Human and physical geography

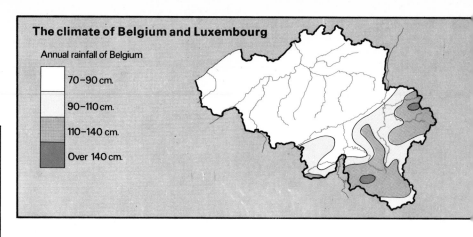

The climate of Belgium and Luxembourg

Annual rainfall of Belgium

- 70–90 cm.
- 90–110 cm.
- 110–140 cm.
- Over 140 cm.

FACTS AND FIGURES: BELGIUM

Full title: Royaume de Belgique (French). Koninkrijk België (Dutch).
Position: Between 2 and 6 E and 49, 50 and 51 50 N. Borders on France, the Duchy of Luxembourg, West Germany and the Netherlands.
Capital: Brussels.
Area: 30,506 sq. km. (11,778 sq. miles).
Population: 9,727,000 (1972). 5,478,000 are Flemish (Dutch speaking). 3,117,000 are Walloon (French speaking). Greater Brussels, which is officially bilingual, has a population of 1,071,000.
Languages: French, Dutch and German are all official languages.
Religion: Most Belgians are Roman Catholics. There are about 24,000 Protestants and 35,000 Jews.
Political system: A parliamentary democracy in which all Belgian men and women, over the age of 21, have the right to vote.
Armed forces: Total: approx. 94,000. Compulsory service lasts for 12 months for privates and 15 months for voluntary reserve officers.

The climate of Belgium is, on the whole, temperate and similar to that of Britain. The average rainfall is about 83 cm. (32 inches), but it is much higher in the hilly Ardennes region of the south east. Early winter is usually the wettest time of the year. Belgians are very conscious of the drizzle, which seems so often to fall, and *"La drache nationale"* has become a national joke. Fog and mist are common in the damp, low-lying areas of Flanders away from the coast, as a result of the cooling of the night air.

Brussels

(Temperature °C; months J F M A M J J A S O N D)

The natural vegetation of Belgium and Luxembourg

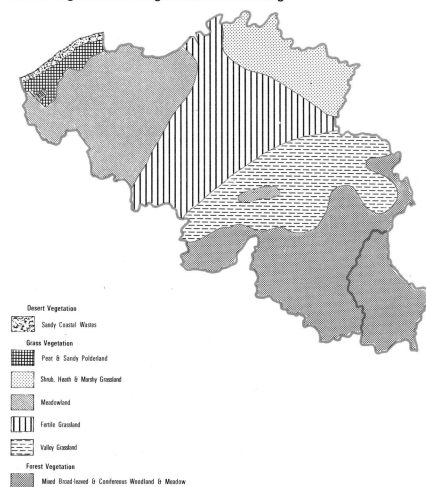

Desert Vegetation
- Sandy Coastal Wastes

Grass Vegetation
- Peat & Sandy Polderland
- Shrub, Heath & Marshy Grassland
- Meadowland
- Fertile Grassland
- Valley Grassland

Forest Vegetation
- Mixed Broad-leaved & Coniferous Woodland & Meadow

FACTS AND FIGURES: LUXEMBOURG

Full title: Grand Duché de Luxembourg.
Position: Approx. 6 E and between 49 50 and 50 20 N. The Grand Duchy of Luxembourg must not be confused with the Belgian province of Luxembourg.
Capital: Luxembourg City.
Area: 2,586 sq. km. (999 sq. miles).
Population: 352,000 (1973). The capital has a population of 78,300.
Language: Luxemburgish (a German dialect not spoken elsewhere). French, German and English are widely used.
Religion: Roman Catholic. In 1960, there were 2,951 Protestants and 643 Jews.
Political system: A constitutional monarchy. Citizens, over the age of 18, have a right to elect the members of the Chamber of Deputies.
Armed forces: A battalion-sized army of volunteers.

population density

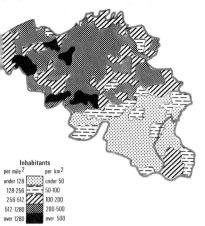

Inhabitants	
per mile²	per km²
under 128	under 50
128-256	50-100
256-512	100-200
512-1280	200-500
over 1280	over 500

...ium is one of the most densely populated ...s of Europe. It has a population density ...ughly 315 people per square kilometre ...per square mile). Of the population ...out 9.7 million, about 600,000 are ...gners. Growing prosperity has resulted ...ge towns gaining at the expense of ...ler townships. Five towns—Brussels, ...verp, Liège, Ghent and Charleroi—have ...over a quarter of the total population. ...Flemish provinces have about 55% of ...opulation and the Walloons 33%. The ...ity of population is twice as great ...ng the Flemings.

The Belgian system of government

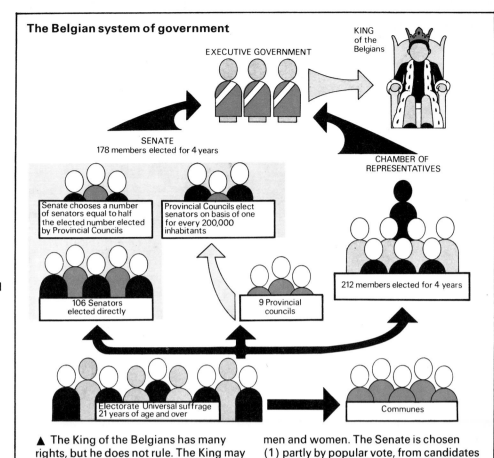

▲ The King of the Belgians has many rights, but he does not rule. The King may dissolve Parliament, and appoint and dismiss ministers. If a government falls, it is his job to find a minister to form a new government. Parliament consists of two Houses, both with similar powers. The House of Representatives is elected by all men and women. The Senate is chosen (1) partly by popular vote, from candidates who belong to bodies such as professional organizations or trade unions; (2) partly from nominations by the Provincial Councils; and (3) partly from nominations by the senators themselves.

opulation of principal towns

72 estimates

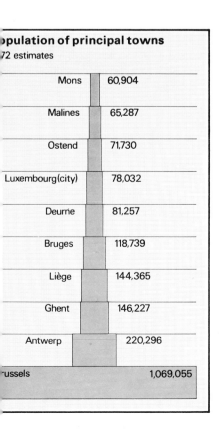

Mons	60,904
Malines	65,287
Ostend	71,730
Luxembourg (city)	78,032
Deurne	81,257
Bruges	118,739
Liège	144,365
Ghent	146,227
Antwerp	220,296
russels	1,069,055

The Luxembourg system of government

▲ The present Grand Duke, Jean, has been sovereign since 1964 when his mother abdicated. The Crown is hereditary in the House of Nassau. The Grand Duke appoints the Prime Minister, whose government must consist of at least three other ministers. Legislative power is in the hands of a Council of State, appointed by the sovereign, and a Chamber of Deputies elected by the people of Luxembourg. Both the Chamber of Deputies and the Duke and his Ministers may submit matters to the Council of State for discussion.

Reference
History

MAIN EVENTS IN HISTORY

B.C.
c. 500	Belgic tribes move into area now known as Belgium.
50	Roman occupation of region after revolt by Ambiorix is crushed.

A.D.
407	Withdrawal of Roman forces. Northern part of country occupied by people of Germanic origin.
c. 500	Merovingian king begins long process of uniting all of Gaul, including Belgian lands.
800	Belgium becomes part of Charlemagne's Holy Roman Empire. Empire breaks up on Charlemagne's death in 814.
843	Treaty of Verdun makes Belgium part of Lotharingia.
879	Lotharingia absorbed by Germany.
9th-12th centuries	Absence of firm rule leads to rise of powerful local rulers.
12th-14th centuries	Flemish towns grow rich and powerful.
1302	Battle of Golden Spurs. Flemish craftsmen defeat the French to preserve independence.
1346	Louis de Mâle becomes Count of Flanders.
1357	Louis invades Brabant and becomes Duke of Brabant.

THE BURGUNDIAN PERIOD
1369	Louis's heiress, Margaret, marries Philip the Bold, Duke of Burgundy.
1384	Margaret inherits Flanders, Antwerp, Malines and territories in France.
1390	Brabant ceded to Duke Philip.
1393	Limburg ceded to Duke Philip.
1404	John the Fearless succeeds as Duke of Burgundy.
1419	Accession of Philip the Good of Burgundy.
1438-56	Bruges, Ghent and Liège forced to surrender many of their liberties.
1443	Philip buys Luxembourg.
1467-77	Reign of Charles the Bold of Burgundy.
1477	Marriage of Charles's daughter, Mary, to Archduke Maximilian.

THE HAPSBURG PERIOD
1482	Death of Mary. Maximilian becomes Regent over possessions in Low Countries.
1486-92	Low Countries subdued, except for bishopric of Liège.
1494	Maximilian's son, Philip the Fair, assumes control in Low Countries.
1500	Charles V, son of Philip, born in Ghent.
1506	Charles succeeds Philip.
1516	Charles V becomes King of Spain.
1529	Charles V inherits Austria.
1537-8	Revolt of Ghent.
1555	Charles V abdicates. Accession of Philip II of Spain.
1555-58	Growing opposition to Spanish troops in Low Countries and to position of Catholic Church.
1559	Margaret of Parma appointed governor.

THE REVOLT OF THE NETHERLANDS
1569	Revolt of the Sea Beggars on Flemish coast.
1572	Sea Beggars capture Brill. Flemish towns badly hit by restriction on seaborne trade.
1576	Antwerp sacked by Spanish mutineers.
1577-87	Spaniards re-establish authority.
1598	Death of Philip II. Flanders acquires semi-independence.
1648	Peace of Münster. Dutch retain Flemish Zealand and North Brabant and declare the Scheldt closed.

BELGIUM AS A BATTLEGROUND
1667-8	War of Devolution. French capture Tournai.
1679-84	Louis XIV annexes Walloon Flanders and half of Hainaut.
1692	Namur captured by French. Retaken in 1695.
1702-13	War of Spanish Succession. Belated efforts by Spanish to improve conditions in Low Countries hampered by campaigns of Marlborough and Prince Eugene.
1713	French abandon claim on the Southern Netherlands to Austria.
1740-48	War of Austrian Succession.
1747	Belgium occupied by the French. Restored to Austria by Treaty of Aix-la-Chapelle.
1790	All the provinces, except Luxembourg, declare independence from Austria, under title of "United States of Belgium". Collapses after two years.
1794	Following defeat of Austrians, Belgium is incorporated into French Republic.
1804-14	Reign of Napoleon I. Scheldt re-opened to shipping, and French legal code introduced.
1814	Treaty of London. Belgium and Luxembourg united with Netherlands under Dutch King.
1815	Battle of Waterloo. William I crowned King of United Netherlands in Brussels.
1830	Belgian revolt against pro-D policies of William I. Independence of Belgium is recognised by Great Powers.

THE KINGDOM OF BELGIUM
1831	Leopold of Saxe-Coburg is crowned King of the Belgian Dutch refuse to recognise ne Kingdom. French forces calle to expel Dutch from Antwerp
1838	Dutch agree to recognise independence of Belgium.
1839	Treaty of London. Independe and neutrality of Belgium is guaranteed. Belgium surrend parts of N. Flanders and Limburg to Netherlands.
1861-3	Belgium makes free trade agr ments with several nations.
1863	Belgium buys right of free navigation on Scheldt from Netherlands.
1865	Death of Leopold I. Accessio Leopold II.
1878	Leopold's interest in colonies leads to formation of committ to study problems of the Con
1881	Leopoldville established in th Congo.
1885	Congo becomes a new State, a private venture by the King.
1908	Congo becomes a Belgian colony.
1909	Death of Leopold II. Accessio of his nephew, Albert I.

WORLD WAR I
1914	Aug. 4: Germany invades Belgium. Aug. 20: German troops ente Brussels. Aug. 23: Battle of Mons. Oct. 9: Antwerp surrenders. Oct. 30-Nov. 24: First Battle Ypres.
1918	Nov. 22: Albert I and Belgian troops re-enter Brussels after withdrawal of Germans.

BETWEEN THE WARS
1926	Locarno Treaty guarantees Belgian frontiers.
1934	Feb. 17: Death of Albert I. Accession of Leopold III.
1936	April: Belgium substitutes po of independent action for position of neutrality.
1937	Britain and France promise Belgium assistance if invade

WORLD WAR II
1940	Jan.: Belgium refuses permis for Britain and France to stati forces there, after discovery c German plans to invade Belgi May 10: German forces attac Belgium without warning. Belgium is quickly over-run.

May 28: King makes unconditional surrender. Belgian Government forms Government-in-exile. British, Canadian and allied troops are given task of recapturing Antwerp and advancing into Belgium.
Sept. 3: Brussels liberated. Government-in-exile returns, Sept. 8th.
May: Unconditional surrender of Germany.

NTS SINCE 1945

-50 Controversy over future of exiled King Leopold. A referendum favours his return.
Opposition forces King to abdicate. Succeeded by son, Baudouin I.
June: Congo granted independence.
French-speaking faculties of the University of Louvain moved to Ottignies after language riots.
May: King Baudouin visits Zaïre (Congo) and signs a treaty of friendship and cooperation.

UROPEAN UNITY

021	Economic Union between Belgium and Luxembourg agreed.
948	Union enlarged to include Netherlands (Benelux).
949	Belgium signs Treaty of London leading to establishment of Council of Europe. Belgium becomes member of North Atlantic Treaty Organization (NATO).
951	Establishment of European Coal and Steel Community between Belgium, France, Italy, West Germany, the Netherlands and Luxembourg.
957	Treaty of Rome brings European Economic Community (Common Market) into being. Belgium joins European Atomic Energy Community (Euratom).
967	Belgium offers home to NATO and SHAPE.
968	Headquarters of Common Market, Euratom, and Iron and Steel Community grouped in Brussels.

The Arts

LITERATURE

Conscience, Hendrick (1812-83). Revived literary Flemish: *The Lion of Flanders*.
Pirmez, Octave (1823-83). Mystical meditations: *Les Heures de Philosophie*.
De Coster, Charles (1827-79). Novelist: *La Légende de Uylenspiegel*.
Gezelle, Guido (1830-99). Lyric poet who wrote in Dutch.
Verhaeren, Emile (1855-1916). Poet: *La Ville Tentaculaire*.
Pirenne, Henri (1862-1949). Historian of international fame.
Maeterlinck, Maurice (1862-1916). Nobel prizewinner: *The Blue-bird, Pelléas et Mélisande*.
Lateur, Frank (Stijn Steuvels) (1871-). *De Vlaschaard*.
Woestijne, Karl van de (1878-1929). Poet and essayist.
Feirlinck, H. (1879-1967). Novelist: *Het Gevecht met de Engel*.
Plisnier, Charles (1896-1952). Short stories and novels in French: *Faux Passeports*.
Ghilderode, Michel de (1899-1962). Dramatist: *Fastes d'Enfer*.
Goris, Jan-Albert (Marnix Gijsen) (1889-). Novels, poems and essays in Dutch.
Simenon, Georges (1903-). Novelist. Creator of the Maigret detective novels.
Boon, Louis Paul (1912-). Novelist who sympathizes with the outsider in society.
Mallet-Joris, Françoise (1930-). Novelist. Won Femina Prize, 1958.

PAINTING

Van Eyck, Jan (1365-1440). Flemish artist who developed the use of oil painting. Major works include the Ghent altarpiece and *Portrait of Giovanni Arnolfini and wife*.
Van Eyck, Hubert (c. 1366-1426). Central panel of Ghent altarpiece, *Adoration of the Lamb*.
Flémalle, Master of (perhaps Campin, Robert c. 1378-1444). Mérode altarpiece.
Van der Weyden, Rogier (1399-1464). Altarpieces: *Descent from the Cross, The Seven Sacraments, Last Judgement*.
Bouts, Dirk (c. 1415-75). Altarpiece: *The Holy Sacrament*.
Memling, Hans (1433-94). Paintings on reliquary of St. Ursula.
Bosch, Hieronymus (c. 1450-1516). *The Last Judgement, The Temptation of St. Anthony*. Many paintings for secret Flemish brotherhood.
Massys, Quentin (1466-1530). Introduced Italian influence into Flemish art. *Lamentation over Dead Christ*.
Orley, Bernard van (1488-1541). Cartoons for tapestry: *The Entombment*.

Brueghel, Pieter the Elder (c. 1525-69). Many paintings of contemporary Flemish life, often in protest at Spanish excesses.
Rubens, Paul (1577-1648). Portrait painter and landscape artist. *Adoration of the Magi, Fall of the Damned*.
Jordaens, Jacob (1593-1678). Pictures of merrymaking among gods and common folk.
Van Dyck, Anthony (1599-1641). Portraitist. Court painter to Charles I of England.
Teniers, David, the younger (1610-90). Genre painter.
Redouté, Pierre Joseph (1759-1840). Luxembourg artist, famous for flower-paintings.
Wouters, Rik (1822-1916). Dynamic colours and dematerialized forms.
Pernicke, Constant (1886-1952). Expressionist painter who specialized in Flemish peasants and landscapes.
Ensor, James (1860-1949). Expressionist painter: *Entry of Christ into Brussels*.
Masereel, Franz (1889-). Specialized in woodcuts.
Magritte, René (1898-). Surrealist artist.

ARCHITECTURE AND DECORATIVE ARTS

Vriendt, Cornelis de (1514-75). Antwerp town hall, choir screen of Tournai cathedral.
Meunier, Constantin (1831-1905). Sculptor who rebelled against classical tradition: *The Hammerman*.
Velde, Henry van der (1863-1957). Leader of "art nouveau" movement.
Horta, Baron Victor (1861-1947). Prominent in "art nouveau" movement.
Minne, George (1866-1941). Leading figure in "art nouveau" movement.

MUSIC

Binchois, Gilles (c. 1400-60). Rondeaux and hymns.
Dufay, Guillaume (c. 1400-74). Motets and hymns.
Prés, Josquin des (c. 1450-1521). Motets, masses and songs.
Willaert, Adrian (1490-1562). Madrigals, motets and songs.
Lassus, Roland de (c. 1562-94). Psalms and secular music.
Grétry, André (1741-1813). Light operas: *Zémire et Azor*.
Franck, César (1822-90). Symphonies and piano works.
Lekue, Guillaume (1870-94). Outstanding pupil of César Franck.

CINEMA PRODUCERS

Feyder, Jacques (1888-1948). Work includes *La Kermesse Heroïque*.
Rouleau, Raymond (1904-). Produced *The Witches of Salem*.

Agriculture in Belgium and Luxembourg

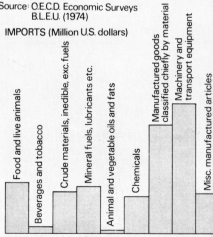

FACTS AND FIGURES: BELGIUM

Total wealth produced: 1,583·1 billion Belgian francs (£19.3 billion).

Economic growth rate: 5.2% (5 year average, 1968-72) at 1970 prices.

Main sources of income:
Agriculture: Flax, market-gardening (fine vegetables and flowers), sugar beet.
Industry: Steel, glass, textiles, machinery and machine tools, chemicals, cut diamonds.

Main trading partners: Common Market countries, other Western European countries, and the U.S.A.

Currency: £1=82 Belgian francs (1975, approx).

Budget:
Revenue: 446.7 billion BFr. (1972).
Expenditure: 436.8 billion BFr.
(Communications: 102 billion BFr;
Education: 111 billion BFr;
Social Services: 73.4 billion BFr;
Defence: 45 billion BFr.)

Wheat

Oats

Barley

Flax

Tobacco

Sugar Beet

Potatoes

Market Gardening

Bulbs

Orchard Fruits

Grapes

Dairy Products

Beef Cattle

Cows

Pigs

Sheep

Principal-Fishing Ports

FACTS AND FIGURES: LUXEMBOURG

Main sources of income:
Agriculture: Potatoes, barley, beet, oats, wheat, wine.
Industry: Steel, chemicals.

Currency: Fixed at par with Belgian franc. For tourist purposes, Belgian money is freely exchangeable in Luxembourg. The opposite is not the case.

Budget:
Revenue: 14.3 billion Luxembourg francs.
Expenditure: 14.5 billion LFr.
(Defence: 516 million LFr;
Education: 2.2 billion LFr; Social Security: 2.8 billion LFr; Transport and Power: 3.8 billion LFr.)

Main trading partners: Common Market and other Western European countries.

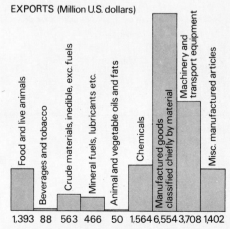

Imports and exports 1972

Source: O.E.C.D. Economic Surveys
B.L.E.U. (1974)

EXPORTS (Million U.S. dollars)

Food and live animals	Beverages and tobacco	Crude materials, inedible, exc. fuels	Mineral fuels, lubricants etc.	Animal and vegetable oils and fats	Chemicals	Manufactured goods classified chiefly by material	Machinery and transport equipment	Misc. manufactured articles
1,393	88	563	466	50	1,564	6,554	3,708	1,402

IMPORTS (Million U.S. dollars)

Food and live animals	Beverages and tobacco	Crude materials, inedible, exc. fuels	Mineral fuels, lubricants etc.	Animal and vegetable oils and fats	Chemicals	Manufactured goods classified chiefly by material	Machinery and transport equipment	Misc. manufactured articles
1,682	225	1,447	1,567	100	1,213	3,636	4,359	1,34

▲ Belgium is an important trading country. She exports about 40 per cent of her total industrial output. At the same time, she has to import many of the raw materials used. Belgium, therefore, has to depend very much upon world markets, and imports and exports are vital to her existence. Luxembourg's trade is less complicated, but her exports are vital to ensure a high standard of living.

Employment in Belgium

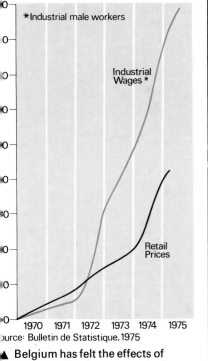

Working population 3,870,000

Agriculture, forestry and fishing
158,000

Industry, transport and building
1,937,000

Armed services (Regular forces) 90,000

Services 1,685,000

Total population 9,727,000

Non-working population
5,857,000

▲ Belgium is a highly industrialized country. A large part of its population is engaged in industry, and it is a mark of a developed country that many people are employed in service industries.

The rise in prices and incomes

*Industrial male workers

Industrial Wages *

Retail Prices

1970 1971 1972 1973 1974 1975

Source: Bulletin de Statistique, 1975

▲ Belgium has felt the effects of inflation, and both wages and prices have soared. The wages of industrial workers have risen more than most. The Government attempted to limit wage rises by controlling price rises in 1975.

Industry in Belgium and Luxembourg

Oostende (Ostend)
Brugge
Antwerpen
Gent
Mechelen
Bruxelles (Brussels)
Liège
Luxembourg

Symbol	Industry
	Major Industrial Centres
	Mechanical Engineering
	Electrical Engineering
	Shipbuilding
	Railway Equipment
	Motor Vehicles
	Motorcycles
	Rubber Products
	Paper
	Furniture
	Leather Goods
	Shoes
	Glass
	Pottery
	Sugar Refineries
	Tobacco Manufacturing
	Principal Coalmining Areas
	Iron & Steel
	Chemicals
	Oil Refineries
	Textile Districts
	Breweries
	Wine
	Diamond Polishing

Goods and services compared to other countries

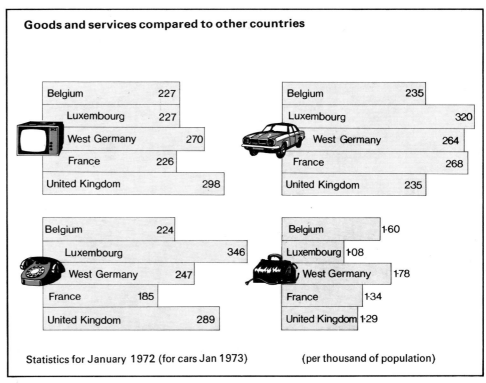

Belgium	227
Luxembourg	227
West Germany	270
France	226
United Kingdom	298

Belgium	235
Luxembourg	320
West Germany	264
France	268
United Kingdom	235

Belgium	224
Luxembourg	346
West Germany	247
France	185
United Kingdom	289

Belgium	1·60
Luxembourg	1·08
West Germany	1·78
France	1·34
United Kingdom	1·29

Statistics for January 1972 (for cars Jan 1973)   (per thousand of population)

Gazetteer

Aalst (50 58N 4 2E). Weaving and brewing centre on R. Dendre. Important for cultivation of hops, and market-gardening. Pop. 46,000.

Antwerp (51 14N 4 23E). Chief Belgian seaport, and major communications centre. Important industries include oil and sugar refining, flour milling and car assembly. Centre of diamond trade. Pop. 217,000.

Ardennes (50 10N 5 40E). High plateau in S.E. Belgium, extending into Luxembourg and France. Fine woodlands, but mainly heath and poor pasture. Centre for sport and hunting. World War II battlegrounds.

Arlon (49 40N 5 47E). One of the oldest towns in Belgium. Roman remains include town wall.

Bastogne (50 0N 5 42E). Rural centre near Luxembourg frontier. Famous for American action in World War II.

Bouillon (49 47N 5 48E). Small Ardennes holiday resort on R. Semoy. Castle of Godfrey of Bouillon overlooks the town.

Bruges (51 13N 3 12E). Most famous of Belgium's medieval towns. Old buildings, canals and bridges make it an important tourist centre. Handmade lace is an important minor industry. Pop. 119,000.

Brussels (50 51N 4 21E). Capital of Belgium. Important commercial and industrial centre. Headquarters of European Economic Community (the Common Market). Many notable buildings in old quarter around Grand' Place. Pop. 1,063,000.

Charleroi (50 28N 4 28E). Major industrial town. Coal mining, steel, iron and glass manufacturing. Heavy electrical engineering. Brewing. Town named after Charles II of Spain.

Courtrai (50 50N 3 15E). Centre of textile industry. Manufactures linen, cotton, nylon, rayon and lace. French defeated in Battle of the Spurs, 1302. Pop. 44,000.

Dinant (50 18N 4 58E). Picturesque tourist centre on R. Meuse. At one time famous for manufacture of copper and brassware.

Esch-sur-Alzette (49 27N 6 00E). Centre of Luxembourg steel industry. Large fertilizer plant. Second largest town in the Duchy. Pop. 27,000.

Ettelbruck (49 51N 6 5E). Major Luxembourg road and rail centre.

Eupen (50 38N 6 3E). German-speaking town, ceded to Belgium in 1918. Manufactures woollen goods and cables.

Genk (50 58N 5 30E). Developed rapidly after World War I, following opening of neighbouring coalfields. Population includes many foreigners who work in mines. Manufactures heavy mining machinery. Pop. 59,000.

Ghent (51 4N 3 43E). One of the most important of Belgium's medieval cities. Many art treasures. Opening of ship canal has made it a major port. Industries include textiles, chemicals, glassware, paper and sugar refining. Pop. 144,000.

Hasselt (50 56N 5 20E). Developed industrially as result of opening of Campine coalfields. Important grain and cattle markets. Brewing and distilling. Tobacco and chicory are cultivated in district. Pop. 40,000.

Huy (50 51N 5 15E). On R. Meuse. Obtained one of the first civic charters in Europe. Famous as home of Peter the Hermit, who proposed the first Crusade.

Liège (50 39N 5 34E). University town and important cultural centre of French-speaking Belgium. Major industrial town. Centre of Belgian metal and armament industries, depending upon coal and iron of neighbourhood, and good transport facilities. Pop. 143,000.

Lier (51 8N 4 32E). Ancient commercial town. Agricultural centre, with small textile industry. Centre of the Flemish political movement. *Liersche Vlaaien* (cooked pastries) speciality of town. Pop. 28,000.

Louvain (50 53N 4 41E). Ancient university town. Famous medieval town-hall. Centre of agricultural district. Industries include brewing and engineering. Pop. 31,000.

Luxembourg City (49 36N 6 7E). Capital of Grand Duchy of Luxembourg. Built on plateau surrounding ravine through which flows R. Alzette. Home of some international bodies, including the European Court of Justice, European Monetary Fund, European Parliament (shared with Strasbourg). Pop. 78,000.

Malines (51 2N 4 27E). Tourist centre with many interesting buildings. Cathedral famous for carillon of bells and its Van Dyck painting of Crucifixion. Once famous for lace-making. Important market-gardening centre. Industries include engineering and car-assembly. Pop. 65,000.

Malmédy (50 26N 6 3E). Small industrial town with tanneries, paper mills and breweries. Ceded by Germany to Belgium after World War I. Almost totally destroyed in fighting in 1944, and now rebuilt.

Mons (50 28E 3 57E). Centre of important coalmining region. Industries include chemicals, brewing, engineering and textiles. Scene of first fighting between British and German armies in World War I. Pop. 62,000.

Namur (50 29N 4 51E). Provincial capital with ancient citadel overlooking junction of Meuse and Sambre rivers. Industries include cutlery, glass, tanning and flour-milling. Pop. 32,000.

Nieuwepoort (51 8N 2 45E). Fishing port at mouth of R. Yser. Yachting harbour. Belgian troops maintained footing in area in World War I, by flooding German trenches.

Ostend (51 13N 3 0E). Principal Belgian fishing port. Important cross-Channel terminal. Harbour for yachts and general shipping. Important holiday resort, with many modern shops, casino and racecourse. Pop. 72,000.

Oudenarde (50 51N 3 37E). Indu town. Brewing, textiles, especially line cotton. Scene of battle in which Marlbo defeated the French, 1708.

Roeselare (50 57N 3 08E). Importan tile factories making linen, lace and ca Centre of the market-gardening, hortic and orchard cultivation in area. Pop. 4C

Ronse (50 45N 3 36E). Textile town. M engaged in weaving cotton and woo manufacture of rayon, but also makes c cotton, woollen and linen goods. 25,000.

St. Hubert (50 2N 5 21E). Ardennes r Church containing the tomb of St. Hu patron saint of hunters. Has become a of pilgrimage.

Saint Niklaas (51 10N 4 09E). Co weaving town, but also manufactures r carpets and hosiery. Market centre o Waasland, a highly productive agricu area reclaimed from the sea. Pop. 49,00C

Spa (50 29N 5 51E). Tourist centre i Ardennes. Famous for its mineral sp. Has given its name to similar spa towns.

Tienen (50 49N 4 56E). Small indu and market town. Trade in beer, grain, and cattle. Cotton and wool spinning. known for its beet-sugar refinery.

Tournai (50 37N 3 23E). Ancient indu town on R. Scheldt. Manufactures ca hosiery, cement and leather goods. Belgian town to be liberated by B troops in World War II. Pop. 33,000.

Turnhout (51 21N 4 47E). Well-know linen-weaving and especially for its fine Canvas and cotton goods also manufact Printing includes manufacture of pl cards. Town Hall was once a palace c Dukes of Brabant. Pop. 38,000.

Verviers (50 36N 5 52E). Eastern western ends of town almost entirely ir trial. Produces large part of Belgi woollen goods. Making of gingerbread speciality, and there is also a choc works. Pop. 32,000.

Veurne (51 5N 2 40E). Flanders t famous for its Procession of the Penit Headquarters town during the Spanish c pation. Now only important as a commu tions centre.

Waterloo (50 45N 4 22E). 17 km (12 m south of Brussels. Scene of battle in w Wellington and Blücher defeated F under Napoleon, 1815.

Ypres (50 52N 2 52E). One of the centres of the medieval cloth trade. Mc industries include engineering and manufacturing. Tobacco is grown in district. Scene of three great battle World War I. Town later rebuilt and an buildings recreated.

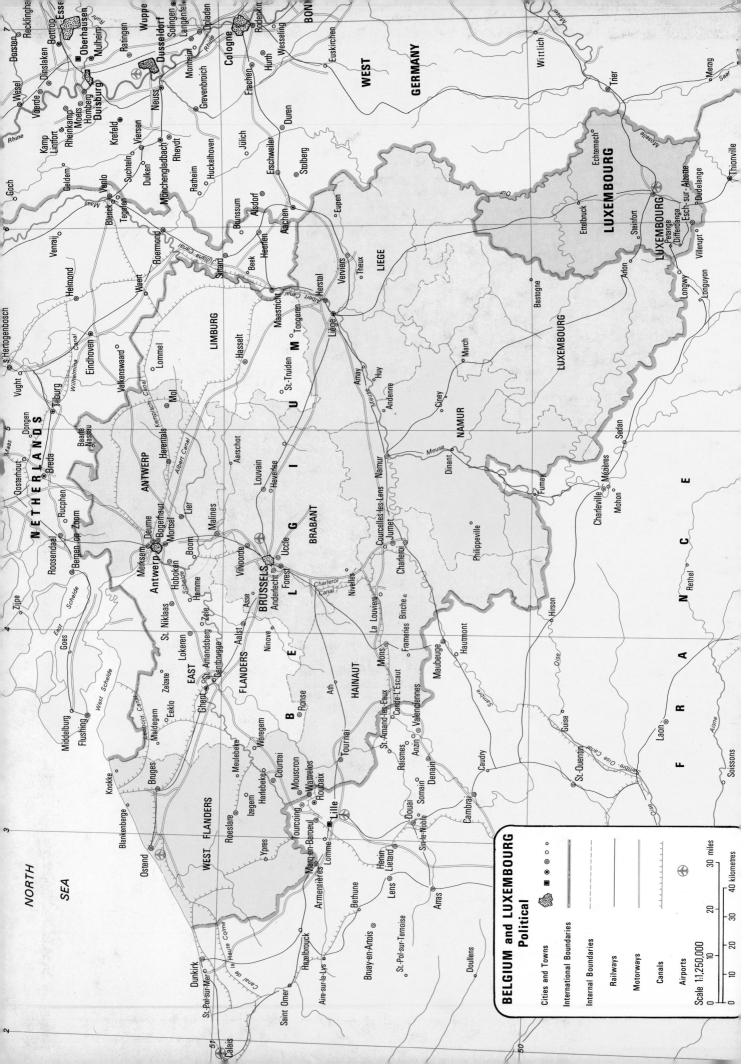